ARTS & CRAFTS PRIMARY 4

Jane Martin

Art consultant:
Lissete Madrazo

Course consultant:
Harriet Thompson

BY ME

My name is:

....

....

....

Contents

Subjects in art

Artists observe the world around them. They choose different subjects for their artwork.

1 Look and write.

1 A person is the subject in a

portrait______.

o r p a t i r t

2 Objects are the subject in a

______ ______.

l s i t l   e f l i

3 An animal is the subject in this

______.

u p c t s l r u e

4 Buildings are the subject in a

______.

p c a y i s e t c

5 Land is the subject in a

______.

e s p l a c a d n

1 

Venetian Beauty, Ricardo de Madrazo y Garreta. (1852-1917)

2 

Still Life with Grapes, Birds, Flowers and Shells, Juan de Espinosa. 17th Century

3 

Black Owl Tile, Pablo Picasso. 1956

4 

Madrid desde el Círculo, Fernando Cobo. 2013

5 

No. 64 Autumn, Beaufays, Liege, Belgium, Izabella Godlewska de Aranda. 20th Century

2 What is your favourite subject in art?

Artists choose a subject and sketch it in their sketchbook. First, plan the subject for the cover of your sketchbook. Then, make and decorate your sketchbook.

1. Fold the paper and make four holes down the centre.

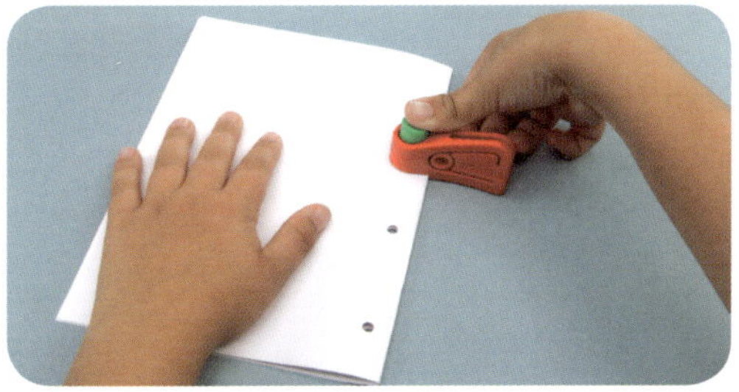

2. Weave wool through the holes and tie the ends.

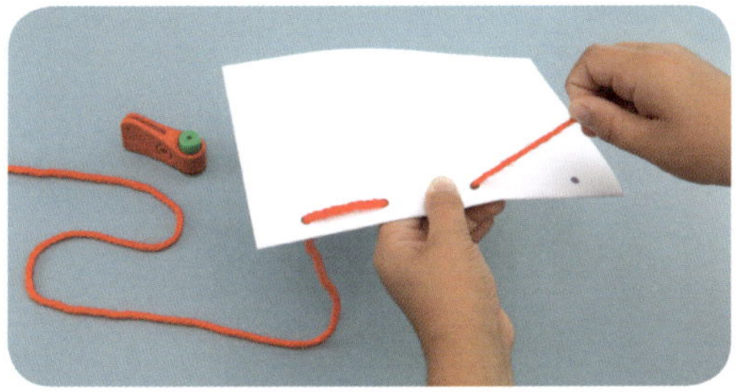

3. Draw and colour your favourite subject on the cover.

My sketchbook design

Finished? Observe your classroom. Draw something in your sketchbook.

1 Still life

Window looking to Panarea, Leon Morrocco. 2000

① How many different patterns can you see in this painting?

② What objects do artists show in a still life?

A still life can show natural and man-made objects such as food, flowers and ceramics.

In this still life, the artist carefully arranged the objects on a table. Then, he painted them with different patterns including:

polka dots, stripes and checks.

Which objects in the still life have these patterns?

2 Activity 1 3 Activity 2

3 Complete the objects with the different patterns. Draw another object and decorate it with all three patterns.

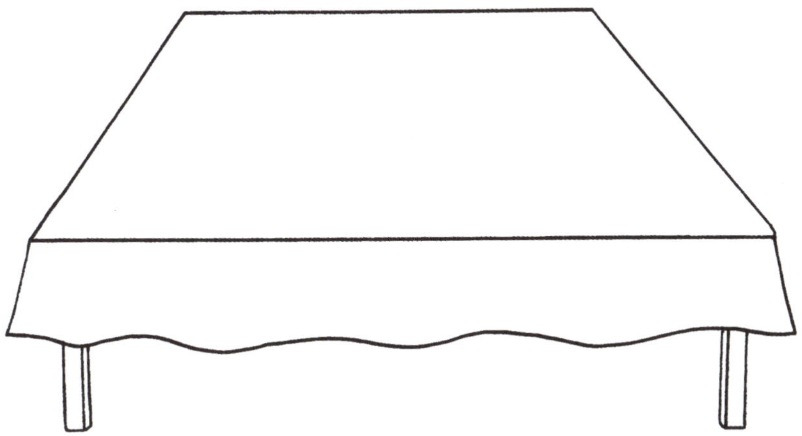

checks

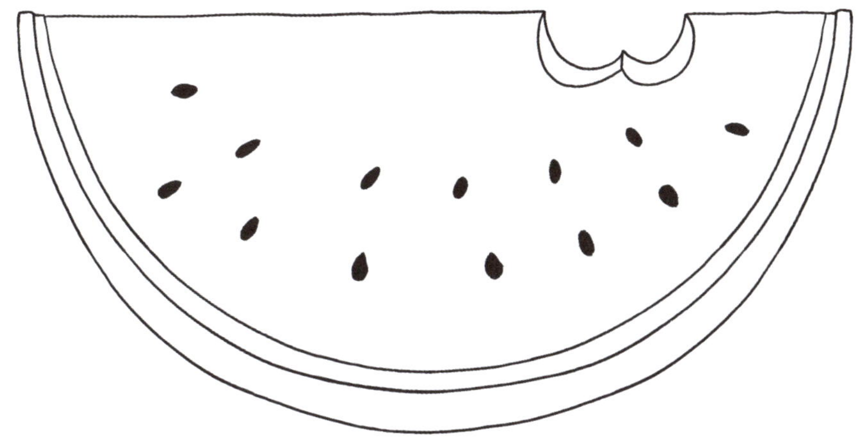

polka dots

stripes

Finished? Find objects with patterns in your classroom and draw them.

Pattern collage

Patterns can be found in natural and man-made objects.

1. Cut out patterns from magazines.

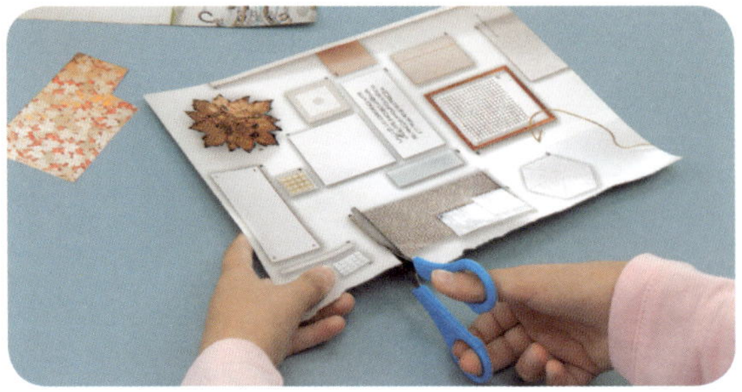

2. Cut out different shapes.

3. Glue the shapes to make a still life.

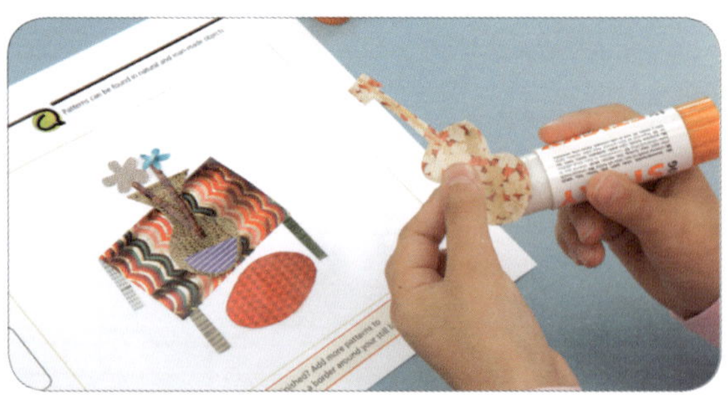

Finished? Add more patterns to make a border around your still life.

Still life patterns

Artists carefully choose and arrange objects for a still life. They can add patterns to make the objects more interesting. What patterns will you use in your still life?

Step 1

Choose and arrange objects for your still life.

Step 2

Observe and draw.

Step 3

Add colourful patterns.

Step 4

Paint.

Finished? Choose a different subject for a still life. Draw and colour it with patterns.

2 Portrait

Girl Selling Fruit, Bartolomé Esteban Murillo. 1650

① Do you think the girl in the painting is happy or sad? Why?

② **How do artists show different emotions in a portrait?**

A portrait is a painting of a person or people. Artists can show different emotions in a portrait.

First, artists use the correct proportion to show the shape, size and position of the parts of the face.

Then, they can express different emotions with the shape of the eyes, eyebrows and mouth.

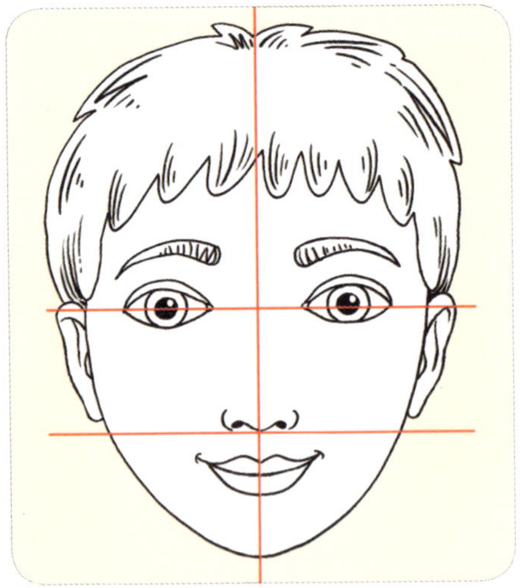

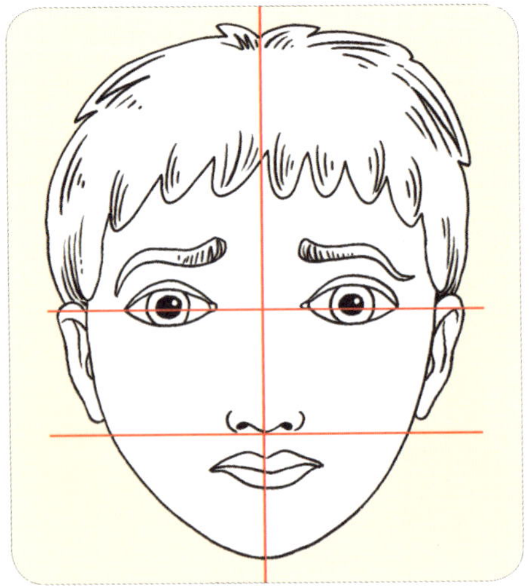

How does this artist show us how the girl feels?

4 Activity 1 5 Activity 2

③ Follow the steps to draw a face with the correct proportion.

A

Draw guidelines:

1. a vertical line down the centre
2. a horizontal line across the centre
3. a horizontal line halfway between line 2 and the chin

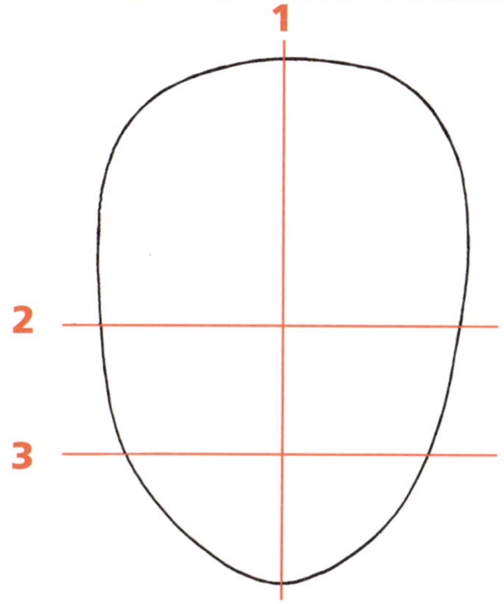

B

Draw the parts of the face:

- the eyes on line 2
- the eyebrows above line 2
- the nose above line 3
- the ears slightly above lines 2 and 3
- the mouth below line 3
- hair on the forehead and around the head

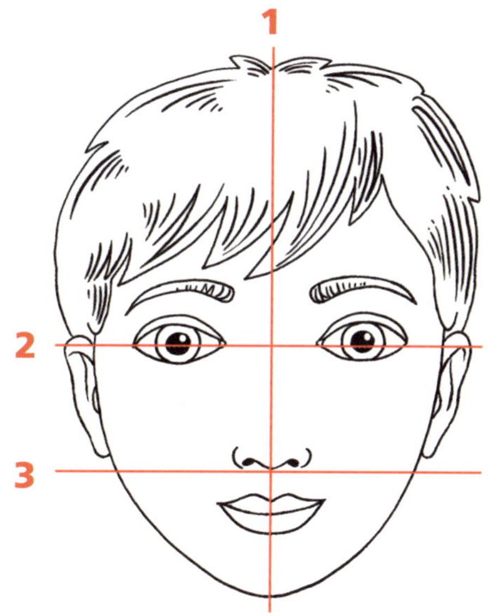

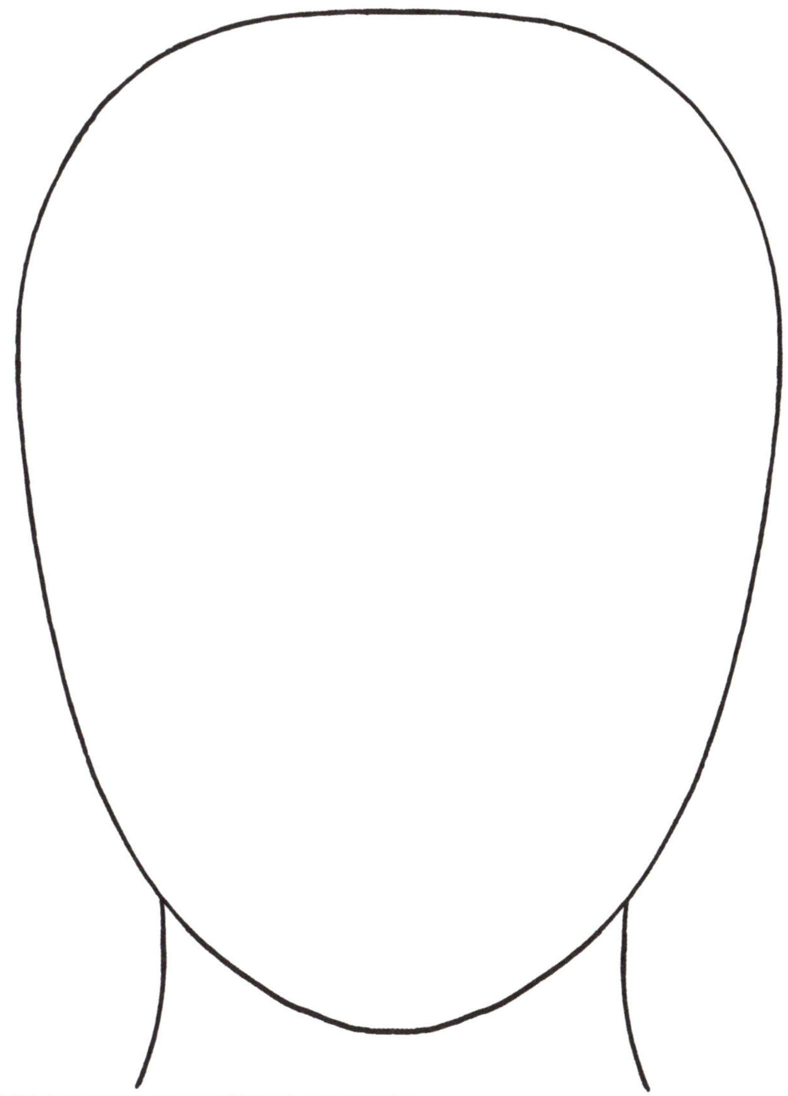

Finished? Erase the guidelines and colour the face.

Expressing emotions

People express emotions with their face. The shape of their eyes, eyebrows and mouth can show how they feel.

1. Draw the eyes and eyebrows to show the emotion.

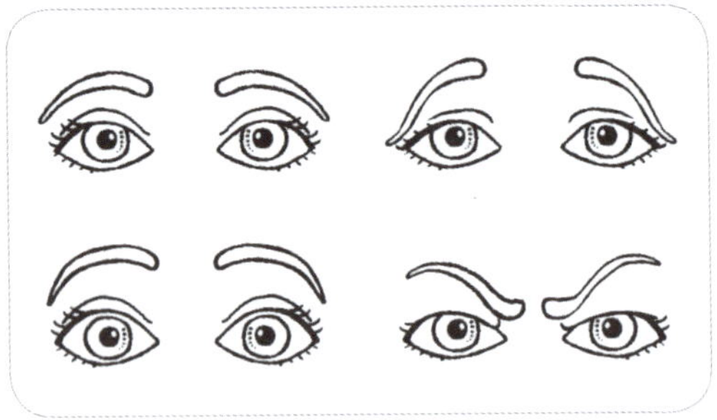

2. Draw the mouth.

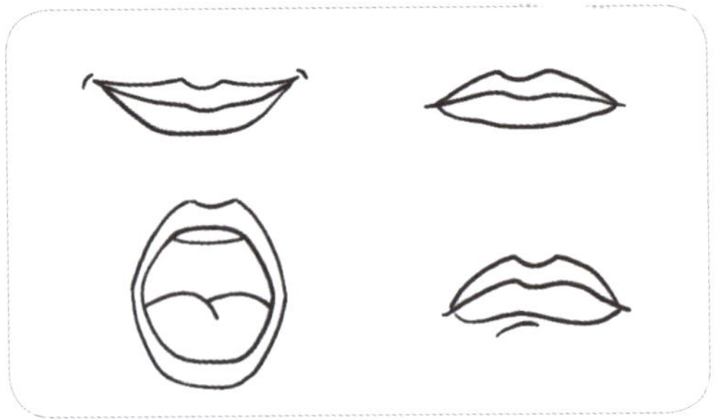

3. Colour the face.

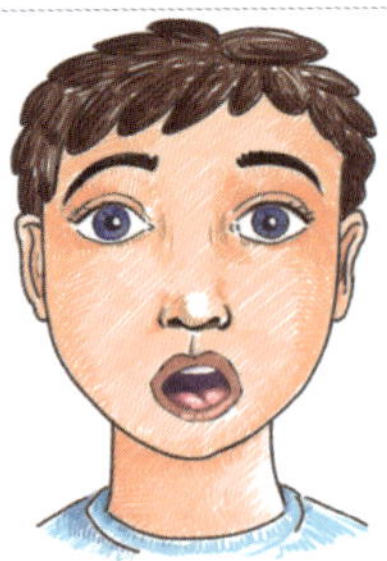

I'm sad.

I'm happy.

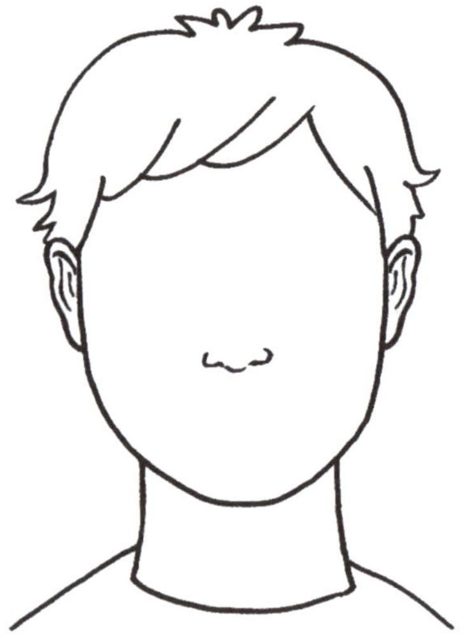

I'm angry.

I'm surprised.

Finished? Draw a face with a different emotion.

Expressive portrait

Portraits can show how a person feels. Think about the different emotions that you feel. Which emotion will you show in your portrait?

Step 1

Draw a head, a neck and shoulders. Add guidelines.

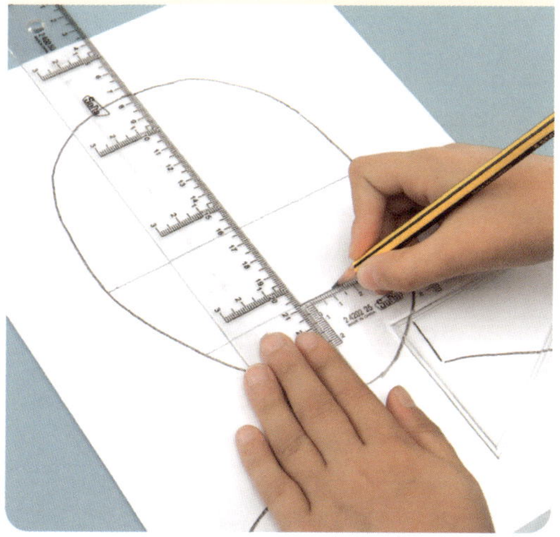

Step 2

Draw the eyes, eyebrows, nose and mouth.

Step 3

Add ears and hair.

Step 4

Erase the guidelines and colour.

Finished? Colour the background with lines, shapes and colours that express that emotion.

3 Dreamtime art

Kangaroo Dreaming with Rainbow Serpent, Michael Nelson Tjakamarra. 1992

1. Which animal can you see in this painting?

2. What types of lines, shapes and colours do artists use in Dreamtime art?

The native people of Australia, the Aborigines, make a special type of art called Dreamtime art. They paint colourful dots, lines and shapes to make symbols of animals, people and other elements from nature. A symbol is an image that represents an object or idea.

This artist paints with two colours on opposite sides of the colour wheel, called complementary colours.

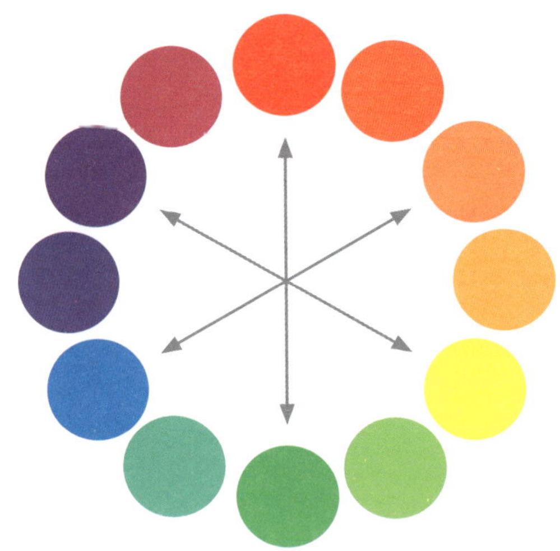

Which two complementary colours does the artist use in this painting?

6 Activity 1 7 Activity 2

3 Colour the complementary colour in each box. Use those colours to colour each animal.

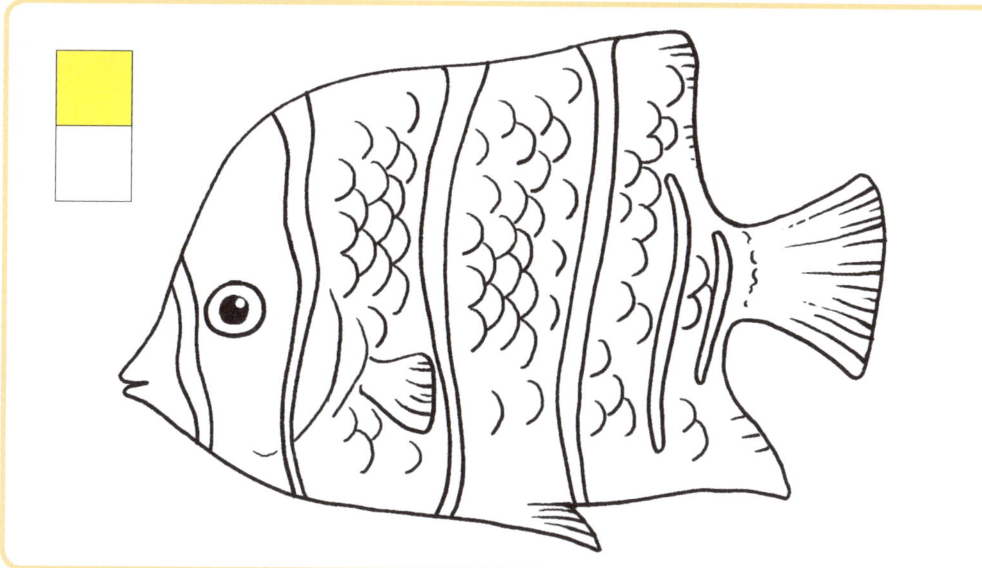

Finished? Draw another animal and colour it with complementary colours.

Symbols

Symbols in Dreamtime art represent animals, people and elements from nature. The artist uses the symbols to tell a story.

spear

animal track

kangaroo track

the Sun

water

campsite

1. Draw three animals.

2. Add symbols to tell a story.

3. Colour with dots and complementary colours.

Finished? Write a short story about your artwork.

Australian boomerang

The Australian aborigines invented a tool for hunting called a boomerang. It is a curved piece of wood that spins through the air. Today, children play games with boomerangs of different shapes.

Step 1

Trace the boomerang template onto cardboard. Cut out.

Step 2

Draw and colour animals on the boomerang.

Step 3

Add symbols and dots with complementary colours.

Step 4

Bend the sides upwards.

Finished? Draw around your hand. Decorate it with symbols, dots and complementary colours.

Template page 65

REVIEW 1 Stained glass windows

Window depicting the Magi on Horseback, Canterbury Cathedral. 13th Century

1 What are the people in this artwork doing?

2 How do artists create stained glass windows?

Stained glass windows are made with small pieces of coloured glass. The artist colours and cuts the glass into different shapes, then puts them together to show people, animals, plants or patterns. Light enters through the window and creates a bright, colourful effect.

Some stained glass windows show important events or tell stories.

What complementary colours can you see in this stained glass window?

9 Activity 1 10 Activity 2

Rose windows

A rose window is a special stained glass window made with patterns of shapes that go around in a circle. The patterns create the shape of a flower.

Step 1

With a compass, draw a circle with a radius of 10 cm.

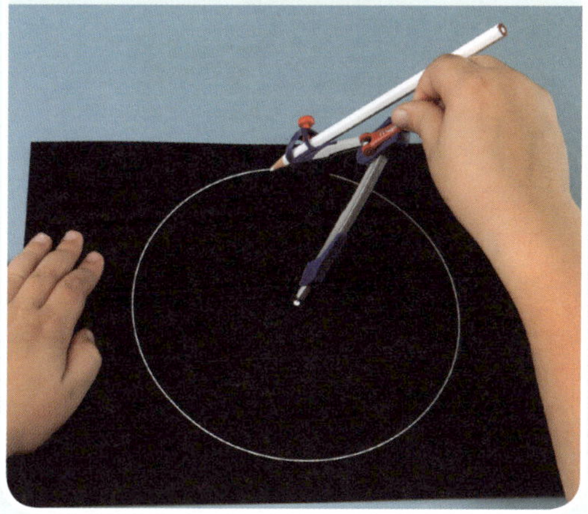

Step 2

Use the compass to divide the circle in six equal parts.

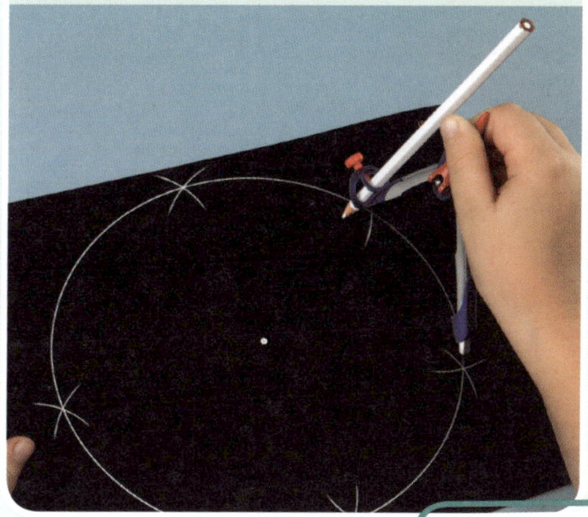

Step 3

Draw lines across the circle with a ruler.
Cut out the circle.

Step 4

Fold the circle on the lines.
Draw and cut out shapes.

Finished? Use your artwork as a stencil. Draw your rose window pattern. Plan the colours you will add.

Template page 67

Circular patterns

The coloured pieces of glass in a rose window are arranged in circular patterns. These patterns can be enjoyed from both inside and outside the building.

Next step: Work together to make a large rose window.

Step 5

Work with your partner and cut out strips of cellophane.

Step 6

Cut out different shapes.

Step 7

Glue the cellophane to make a pattern on one circle.

Step 8

Glue the other circle on top.

Finished? Glue pieces of primary coloured cellophane over some of the shapes to make different colours.

Classroom rose window

1. Make a large rose window on your classroom window.
2. Talk about your rose window.

- How did you make it?
- What shapes did you cut out?
- What colours did you use?
- What patterns are in your artwork?
- Where have you seen a rose window? Describe it.

4 Skyscape

The Starry Night, Vincent van Gogh. 1889

① Which parts of this painting look like they are moving?

② How do artists show movement in a painting?

A skyscape is a painting that mostly shows the sky but can include some land too.

In this nighttime skyscape, the artist painted many lines that show movement in both the land and the sky.

The swirling lines and bright colours make the clouds, stars and moon look like they are moving around the sky.

Swirls, spirals, curved and wavy lines express movement in an artwork.

Which lines can you see in the tree?

11 Activity 1 12 Activity 2

3 Complete the lines in each box to show movement. Then, create your own moving lines.

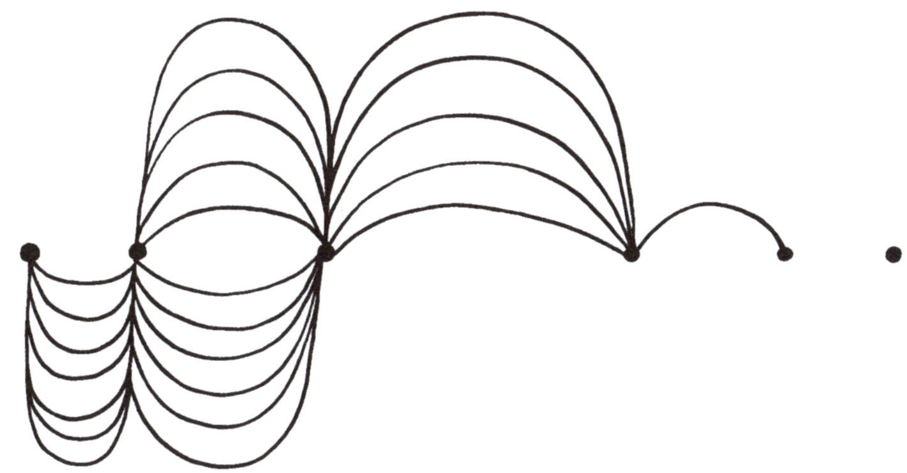

Finished? Colour all the lines.

Continuous lines

Artists can draw long, continuous lines that move all around the picture.

1. Complete the line for the sky.

2. Complete the line for the land.

3. Colour your skyscape.

Finished? Add more lines to show motion.

My starry night

The sky is full of objects that move. Some of these objects shine brightly at night. What lines, shapes and colours will you show in your night sky?

Step 1

Draw the land and sky with a variety of lines and colours.

Step 2

Add natural and man-made features to your landscape.

Step 3

Paint the skyscape.

Finished? Draw and colour a daytime skyscape.

5 Reflection

Hall of the Ambassadors, Alhambra Palace, Granada,
Joaquín Sorolla y Bastida. 1909

(1) How is the building different from its reflection?

(2) How do artists show reflections in a painting?

Water can act like a mirror. It reflects light and images. This painting shows the reflection of a building.

The reflection is upside down and symmetrical to the building. The imaginary line between the building and the water is called the axis of symmetry.

The reflection of an object in water is not as clear as the real object. Artists blend colours and show fewer details in the reflection.

How are the reflections in the photograph and the painting different?

13 Activity 1 14 Activity 2

3 Draw and colour the reflection of the fountain in the water.

Finished? Practise another way to show reflections.

Symmetry in reflection

If a building is symmetrical, an artist uses two lines of symmetry to show its reflection: a vertical axis down the centre of the building and a horizontal axis to show the reflection.

1. Draw and colour the other half of the building.

2. Draw and colour the other half of the reflection.

3. Blend the colours in the reflection.

Finished? Imagine looking in a pond and draw the reflection of your face.

Reflection around us

Water reflects images of many different structures. What type of structure will you choose? How many lines of symmetry will your artwork have?

Step 1

Fold your paper in half. Draw a structure on the top half.

Step 2

Colour the picture except for the sky.

Step 3

Fold the paper and rub.

Step 4

Paint the sky and the reflection.

Finished? Draw and colour a reflection of a structure at night.

6 Recycled art

Bird Band, Tom Every. 1980

1. What materials did the artist use in this artwork?

2. What type of recyclable materials can artists use to create art?

Some artists create art by recycling everyday objects made from plastic, wood, glass and metal.

This artist collected parts of old machines and musical instruments. Using his imagination, he mixed these forms together to create sculptures of birds.

Forms are three-dimensional objects that have volume. They can be geometric or organic. Geometric forms include:

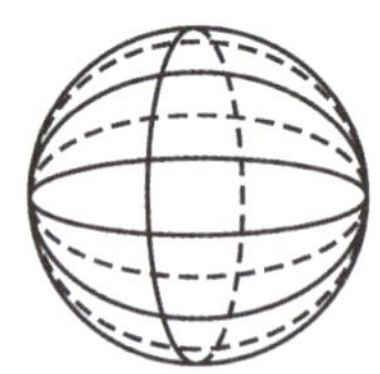

sphere

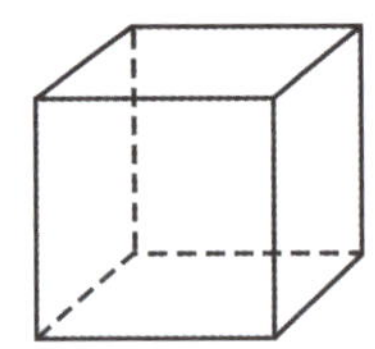

cube

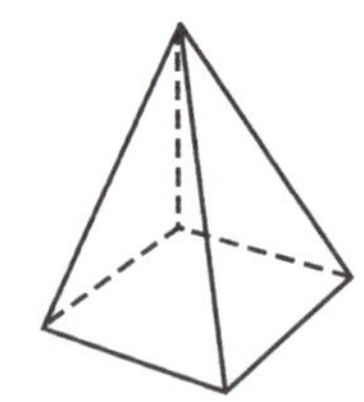

pyramid

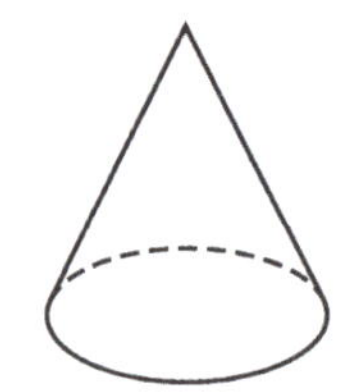

cone

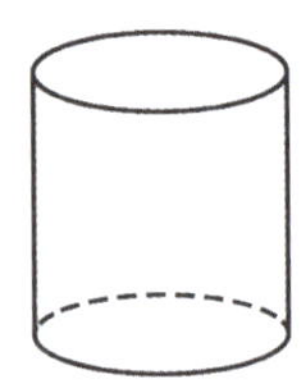

cylinder

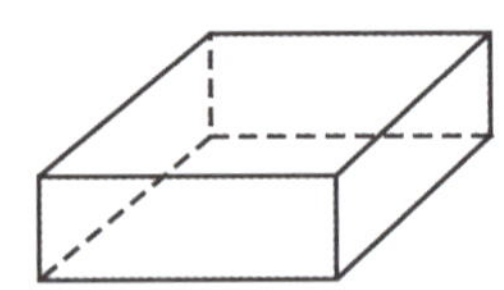

rectangular prism

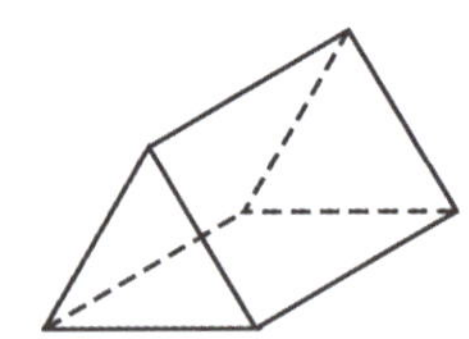

triangular prism

What type of musical instrument can you see in this sculpture?

16 Activity 1 17 Activity 2

3 Connect the shapes to make the forms of these musical instruments. Then, draw your favourite instrument.

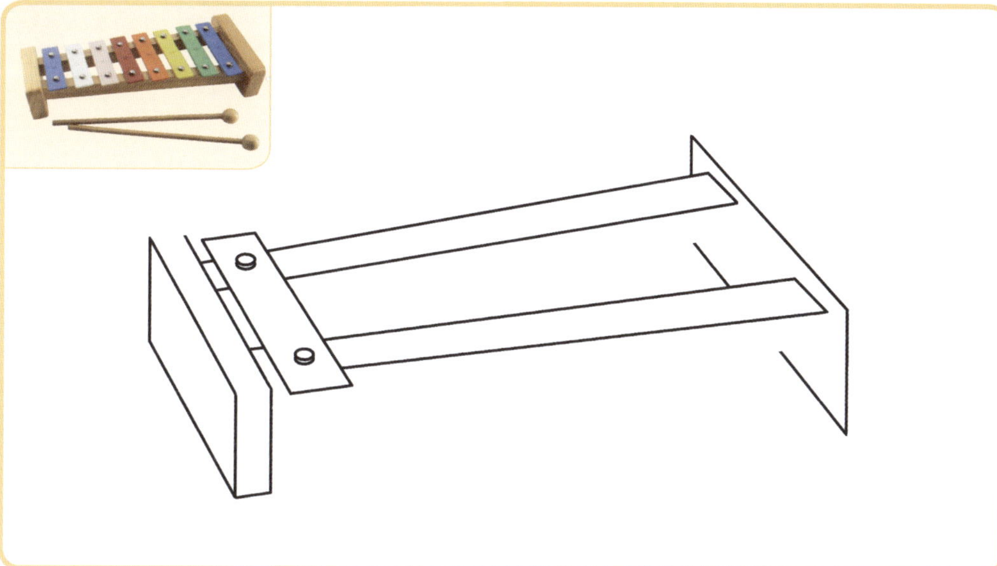

Finished? Add details to each instrument and colour.

Musical machine

Artists draw different forms that show height, width and depth. They also use light and dark colours to show volume.

1. Use forms to invent a new musical machine.

2. Add details.

3. Colour with light and dark colours.

Finished? Draw a background for your machine.

My bird orchestra

Artists use their imagination and recycle objects to make new forms of art. You can make your own bird orchestra with recyclable materials. What materials will you use?

Step 1

Make a bird with recyclable materials.

Step 2

Add details with more recyclable materials.

Step 3

Flatten a straw and make two cuts at one end.

Step 4

Tape the straw inside your bird.

Finished? Arrange your bird sculptures to create a class bird orchestra.

REVIEW 2 Hot-air balloons

Hot-air balloons flying.

① How do hot-air balloons move through the air?

② **What are the different parts of a hot-air balloon?**

The first hot-air balloon was invented in 1783 and had the form of a sphere. Later, the form of the balloon was changed to hold more hot air.

The hot air from the burners makes the balloon rise and float gently in the air with the wind. The basket is light but strong so that people can stand inside.

Hot-air balloons are very colourful and are often decorated with many different lines, shapes and patterns.

Which hot-air balloons have a symmetrical design in this photo?

18 Activity 1 19 Activity 2

Papier-mâché

You can make a model of a hot-air balloon using a technique called *papier-mâché.* Cover a balloon with paper and glue. As the paper dries, it keeps the form of the balloon.

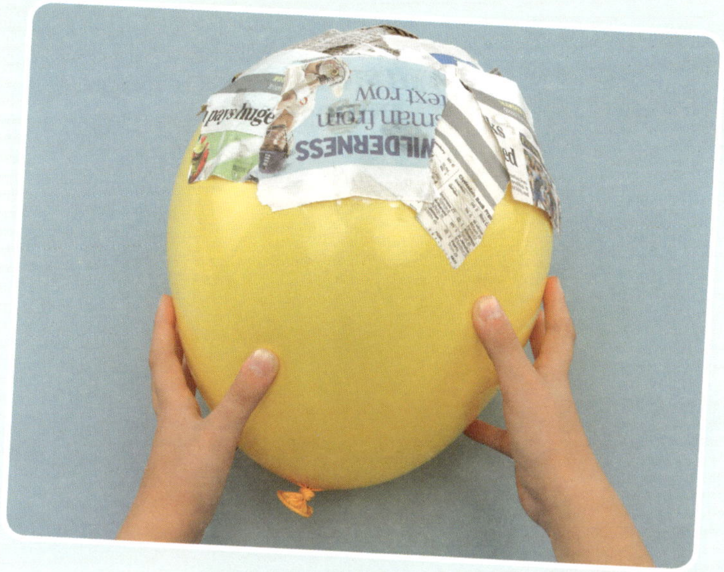

Step 1

Blow up a balloon.
Tape it to a cup.

Step 2

Tear up strips of newspaper and paper towels.

Step 3

Glue two layers of newspaper on the balloon.

Step 4

Glue two layers of paper towels over the newspaper.

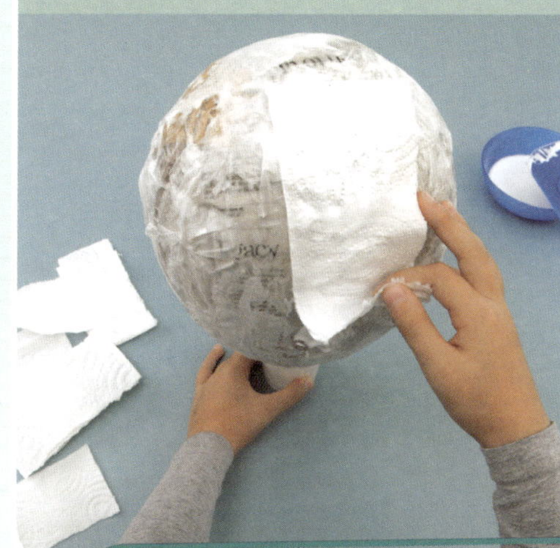

Finished? Plan a design for your balloon.

Colours in the sky

People participate in hot-air balloon races all over the world. These balloons fill the sky with many different colours and designs. What lines, shapes and colours will you use to paint your balloon?

Next step: Work together to organise a hot-air balloon race.

Step 5

Pop the balloon. Make four holes around the bottom and two holes on top.

Step 6

Tie string through all the holes.

Step 7

Paint the balloon.

Step 8

Make a basket and decorate it. Tie it to the balloon.

Finished? Make some figures out of plasticine and put them inside the basket.

1 Hang all the hot-air balloons together.

2 Talk about your hot-air balloon.

- How did you make your balloon?
- What lines, shapes and colours did you use?
- Does your balloon have a symmetrical design?
- How did you make your basket?
- Would you like to fly in a hot-air balloon? Where would you go?

7 Landscape

The Garden, Santiago Rusiñol i Prats. 1908

1 Where do you think this path goes?

2 How do artists use lines to show depth in a landscape?

A landscape is a picture of an outdoor scene. One way artists can create depth in a landscape is by using perspective lines.

They draw two diagonal lines that meet at a vanishing point in the distance. They show objects that overlap and get smaller along the perspective lines.

Which objects get smaller in this garden?

20 Activity 1 21 Activity 2

3 Draw objects along the perspective lines that overlap and get smaller. Complete the neighbourhood garden.

Finished? Draw more objects of different sizes in the garden. Colour.

Diagonal lines

Artists can use many diagonal lines that get closer together in the background to create depth in a landscape.

1. Draw a path.

2. Complete the diagonal lines.

3. Draw objects near and far. Colour.

Finished? Cut out and glue pictures from magazines in your artwork.

The journey

Artists paint landscapes of mountains, countrysides, deserts and forests. They can add paths, roads and railway tracks with perspective lines. Where will the lines in your landscape take you?

Step 1

Draw perspective lines and a background.

Step 2

Draw objects that overlap and get smaller along the perspective lines.

Step 3

Paint the background.

Step 4

Paint the rest of your landscape.

Finished? Cut and glue a traveller in your landscape.

Template page 69

8 Seascape

Oak Tree Beach, Minnie Harms Neebe. 1914

① What different activities are the people doing at the beach?

② How do artists show depth in seascapes?

Artists paint seascapes with a horizontal line to show the horizon. The horizon line is where the sky and the water meet.

They add another line below the horizon to show the shore. The shore is where the water and land meet.

The space between the shore and the horizon creates depth in a seascape.

Artists paint objects near the horizon line smaller to show that they are further away. Artists can also overlap objects to show depth in a seascape.

Can you find the boat that is the furthest away in the painting?

22 Activity 1 23 Activity 2

3 Colour, cut and glue some of the objects along the shore and in the water to show depth in this seascape.

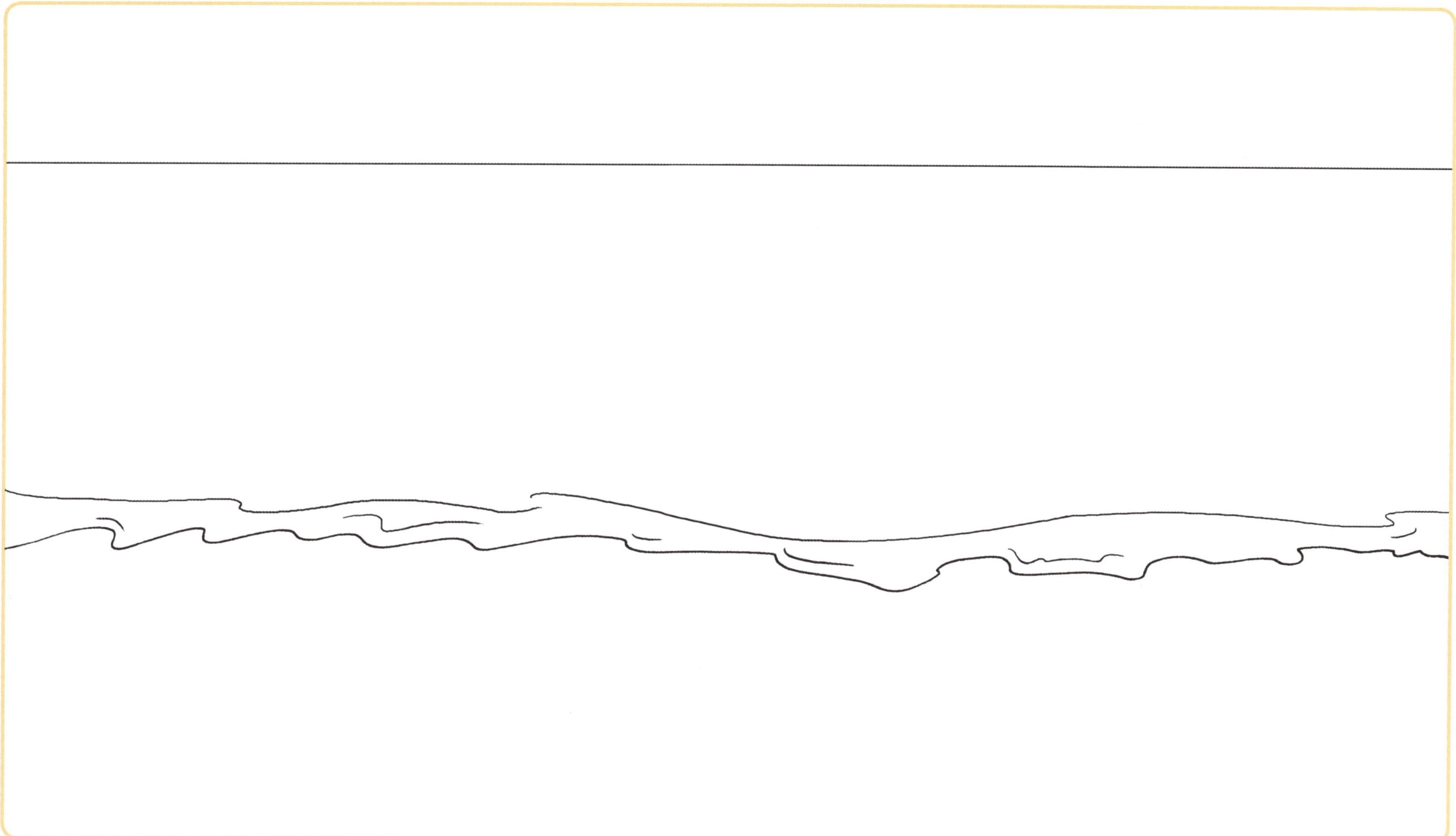

Finished? Draw, colour and cut people, then glue them in your seascape.

Template page 71

Under the sea

Artists can show depth underwater too. They use overlapping and show objects on the sea floor getting smaller and further away.

1. Overlap plants and sea animals in the water.

2. Draw plants and shells of different sizes on the sea floor.

3. Colour your underwater scene.

Finished? Draw a person swimming. Cut and glue the person in your underwater scene.

Silhouette seascape

Artists can show a variety of images in a seascape including boats, trees, shells, balls and umbrellas. What objects will you include in your seascape?

Step 1

Cut out the border.

Step 2

Cut six or seven strips of tissue paper.

Step 3

Glue the strips across the border to show the shore and the horizon.

Step 4

Cut and glue silhouettes that can overlap and get smaller near the horizon.

Finished? Add another silhouette to your seascape.

Template page 73

9 Sculpture

Family Group, Henry Moore. 1945

1 Who are the people in this sculpture?

2 How do artists use positive and negative space in sculptures?

Sculptures are three-dimensional works of art made of forms. They are composed of positive space and negative space.

The form of the family is the positive space in this sculpture. The space between the people is the negative space. The negative space is the empty space inside and around the sculpture.

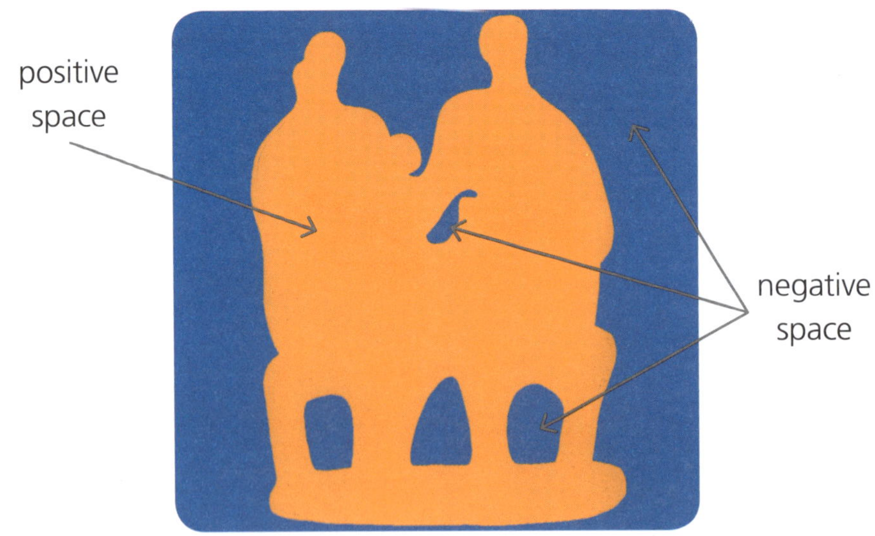

In this sculpture, do you see the positive space or the negative space first?

24 Activity 1 25 Activity 2

3 Colour the columns with designs.

4 Colour the people with details.

Finished? Design a sculpture of your family with positive and negative space.

Negative space

Artists can use a technique called carving to create a sculpture. They take away the negative space to create the final form.

1. Carve around the plasticine.

2. Carve out the plasticine.

3. Draw your sculpture. Colour the positive space.

Finished? Use the plasticine you took away to make another sculpture.

My family sculpture

Another technique used to create sculptures is called moulding. Artists use their hands to mould the positive space of the sculpture. What will the people in your sculpture be doing?

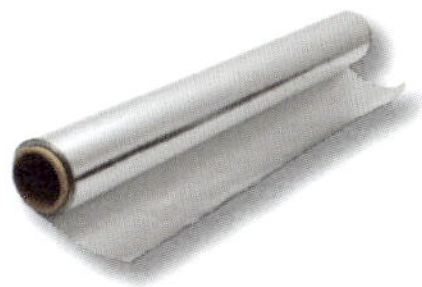

Step 1

Cut two lines at the top and one line at the bottom of the aluminium foil.

Step 2

Gently push the foil together to make the different body parts.

Step 3

Make more figures.

Step 4

Position the figures and glue.

Finished? Mould an object and glue it to your sculpture.

REVIEW 3 Games

Game of Chess, Sofonisba Anguissola. 1555

1 What are the girls doing?

2 What is the subject of this painting?

Artists can combine a variety of subjects in their artwork. This painting shows elements of a portrait, a landscape and a still life.

The painting is a portrait of the artist's three sisters. Each sister is looking at a different sister and the oldest is looking at us.

The girls are playing outside. There are trees nearby and an imaginary landscape in the background.

In the centre of the table there is a still life. The artist shows a chessboard and chess pieces.

What board games do you play with your friends and family?

26 Activity 1 27 Activity 2

Board games

Board games can be set on land, at sea or in an imaginary world. Think of all the art projects you have completed in Arts and Crafts this year. What setting will your board game have?

Step 1

Plan your board.

Step 2

Paint the setting.

Step 3

Add a path.

Finished? Plan the instructions for your game.

How to play

Board games have different rules. Some games have obstacles or questions. Review the information you learned in Arts and Crafts this year. What questions will you ask? What are the rules of your game?

Next step: Work together to organise a class game.

Step 4

Add objects to the board.

Step 5

Write symbols or instructions.

Step 6

Write question cards.

Step 7

Make the game pieces to start playing.

Finished? Write more questions cards with a partner.

Template page 75

Let's play

1. Write the instructions for your game.
2. Talk about your game.

- What is the setting of your game?
- Where do you start and finish?
- What is the goal of your game?
- What are the rules of your game?
- What are the pieces for your game?

Thanksgiving turkey

Autumn is harvest time in many parts of the world. In the United States, people celebrate Thanksgiving to honour the Pilgrims' first harvest. It is a special day to say thank you for the food we eat. Symbols for Thanksgiving include:

Pilgrims and Native Americans

a cornucopia

a turkey

Step 1

Collect a pine cone and some autumn leaves.

Step 2

Glue the leaves on the bottom of the pine cone.

Step 3

Use plasticine to make the face.

Step 4

Add the legs and feet.

Jingle bells

There are many different sounds we associate with Christmas. We can hear the sound of family and friends laughing and talking. We can hear people singing Christmas carols. We can also hear the jingle of Christmas bells.

Step 1

Use clay to make a round base and four coils of increasing size.

Step 2

Attach the smallest coil to the base. Add the longer coils and rub the clay together.

Step 3

Create a design in the clay and make two holes in the top.

Step 4

Let the clay dry. Paint your bell and tie a jingle bell inside it.

Christmas plant

Poinsettias are plants that bloom in December. They are bright red and shaped like a star. This makes them the perfect plant to say Happy Christmas!

Step 1

Colour the biggest leaf with green patterns and the other leaves with red patterns.

Step 2

Fold the leaves along the dotted lines.

Step 3

Put the leaves from biggest to smallest. Push the clip through the centre.

Step 4

Fold a piece of card and push the clip through one half. Write a Christmas message inside.

Template **page 77**

Carnival mask

People celebrate Carnival in many places around the world with music, dancing and parades. They also wear colourful costumes and masks. How will you decorate your Carnival mask?

Step 1

Trace your hands.

Step 2

Cut out the hands and make the holes for the eyes.

Step 3

Glue the hands together and decorate.

Step 4

Add a stick to hold the mask up to your face.

Easter eggs

Easter is a time to celebrate new life. In spring, flowers bloom and birds hatch from eggs. People decorate Easter eggs with different patterns and spring colours.

Step 1

Cut out the eggs and fold each one down the centre.

Step 2

Colour patterns on one side.

Step 3

Fold each egg and rub.

Step 4

Glue the eggs together. Glue them onto a piece of coloured card.

Template page 79

Fireworks

Each town in Spain has a special local festival during summer. The people celebrate with traditional food, music and dance. At night, they light up the sky with fireworks. When is your town's festival?

Step 1

Cover the paper with different shapes and colours.

Step 2

Cover with black paint.

Step 3

Scratch out circles and patterns of colours.

Step 4

Add more fireworks to your night sky.

What is the subject of the artwork?

People, buildings, land, objects... are the subject of the artwork.

It's a...

landscape

portrait

sculpture

seascape

skyscape

still life

There is / There are...

It's got...

I can see a/an...

It shows / They show...

It looks like / They look like...

What's your opinion of the artwork?

I like how the artist painted/used/created/showed...

lines

shapes

patterns

colours

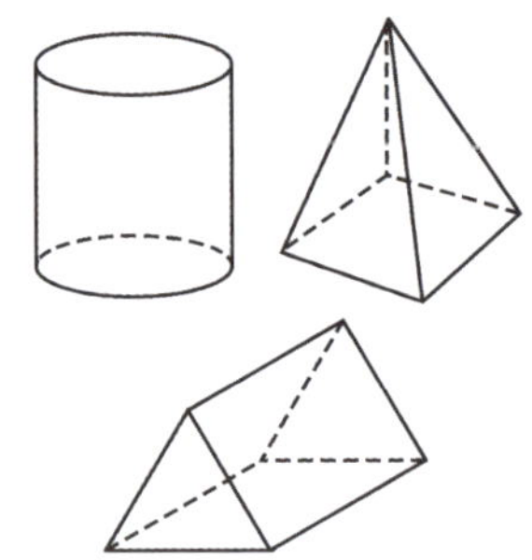
forms

space

depth

movement

symmetry

Art materials

Paper

card | cellophane paper | paper | tissue paper

Glue

glue stick | white glue

Mould

clay | plasticine

Cut

scissors

Draw and colour

coloured pencils | crayons

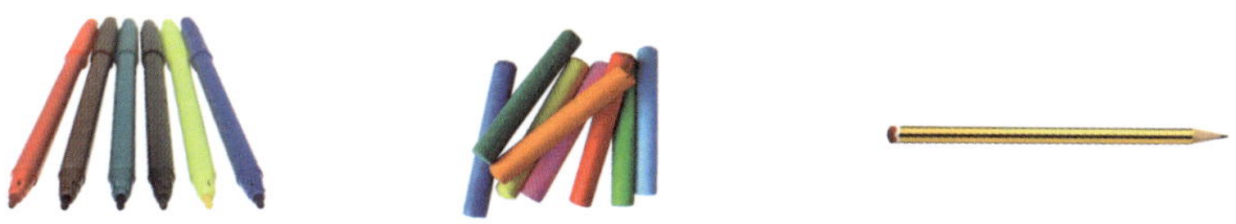

felt tips | oil pastels | pencil

Paint

paintbrush | poster paint | water | watercolours

Extra materials

aluminium foil | balloons | cardboard | clip | compass

glue spatula | leaves | magazine | newspaper | pencil sharpener

pine cone | plastic cup | recycled materials | rubber | ruler

set squares | straws | string | tape | wooden stick | wool

Draw with a pencil

Sketch guidelines lightly so they can easily be erased.

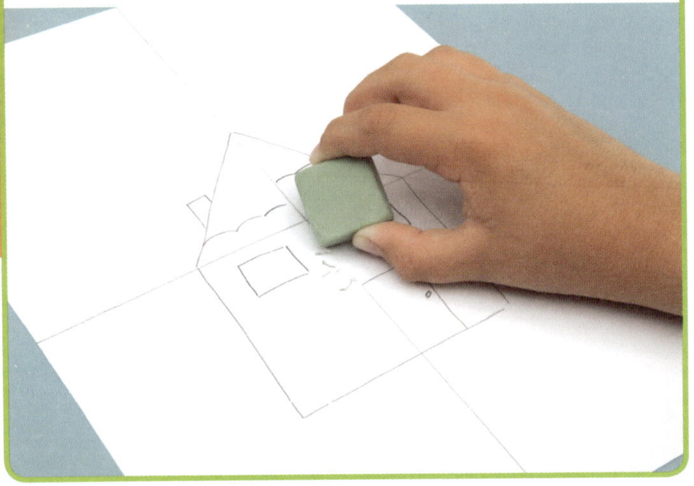

Colour with coloured pencils and crayons

Press soft for light colours and hard for dark colours.

Colour with felt tips

Start with light colours. Then, add darker colours.

Blend with oil pastels

Colour with oil pastels. Blend with your finger, cotton or tissue.

Rub with oil pastels

Colour your picture on half of the paper. Fold the paper and rub with something hard.

Construct with white glue

Place the white glue on one of the objects and hold them together for fifteen seconds.

Draw with a set square

Line up the set square with the edge of the paper.

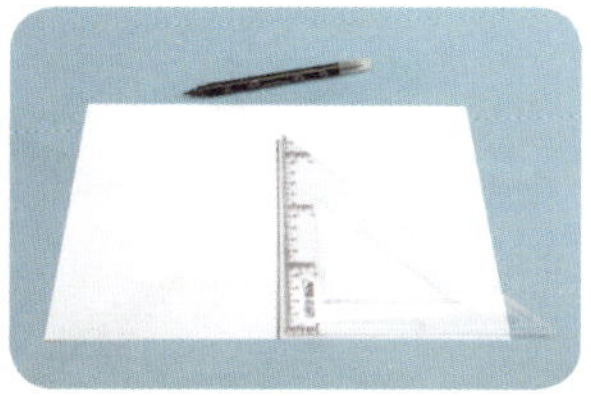

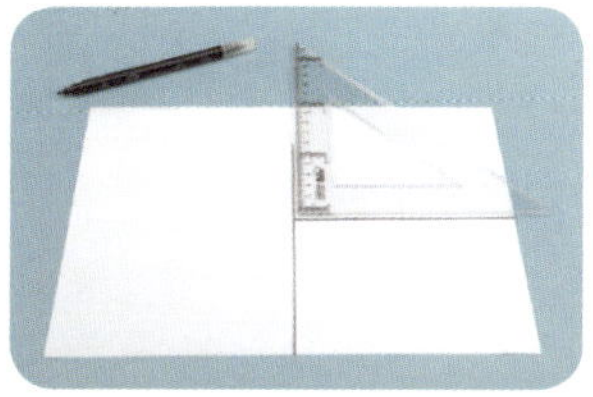

Use it to draw horizontal, diagonal and vertical lines.

Paint with poster paint

Draw a light outline.

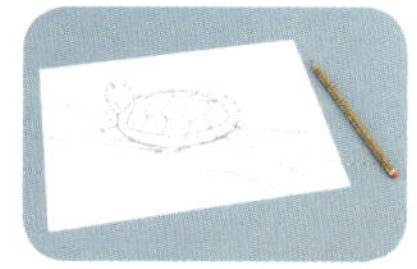

Start with light colours.

Add darker colours.

Carve with plasticine or clay

Cut around the form.

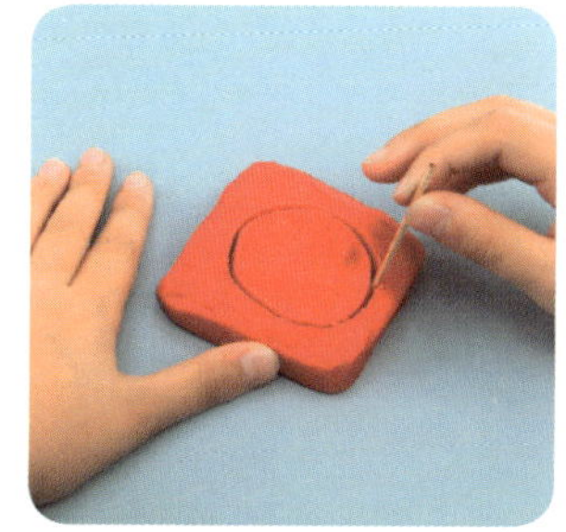

Cut lines and shapes inside the form.

Draw forms

Draw a shape.

Draw an overlapping shape.

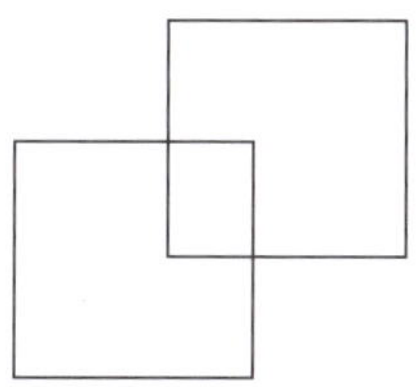

Connect the shapes.

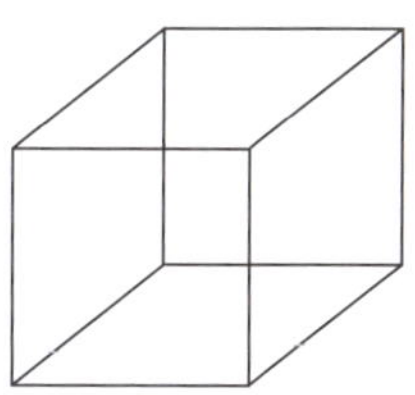

Colour with light and dark colours.

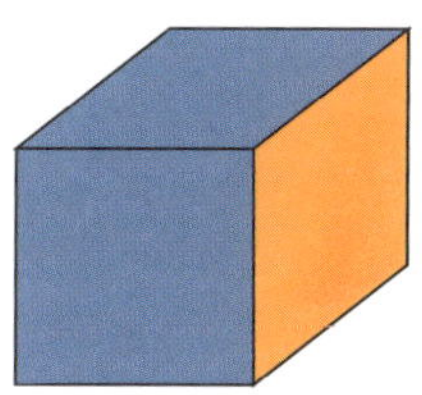

Paint with watercolours

Add more water for lighter colours.

Add less water for darker colours.

Paint lightly over crayon or oil pastel.

Mould with plasticine or clay

Gently mould the form with your hands.

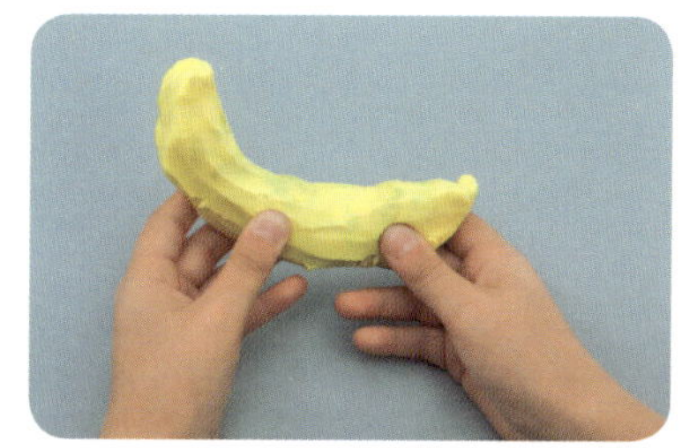

Mix colours.

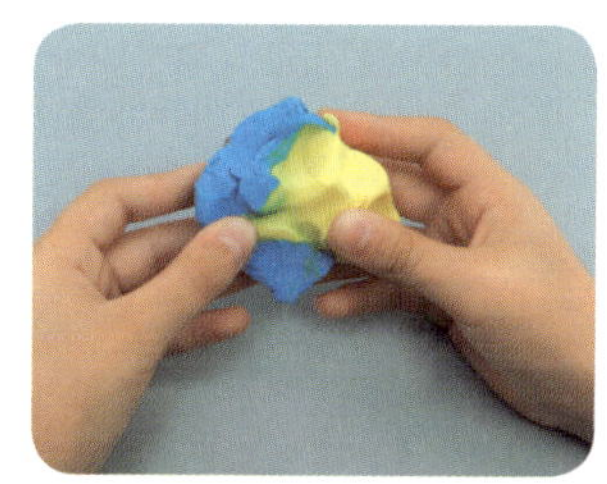

Blend colours.

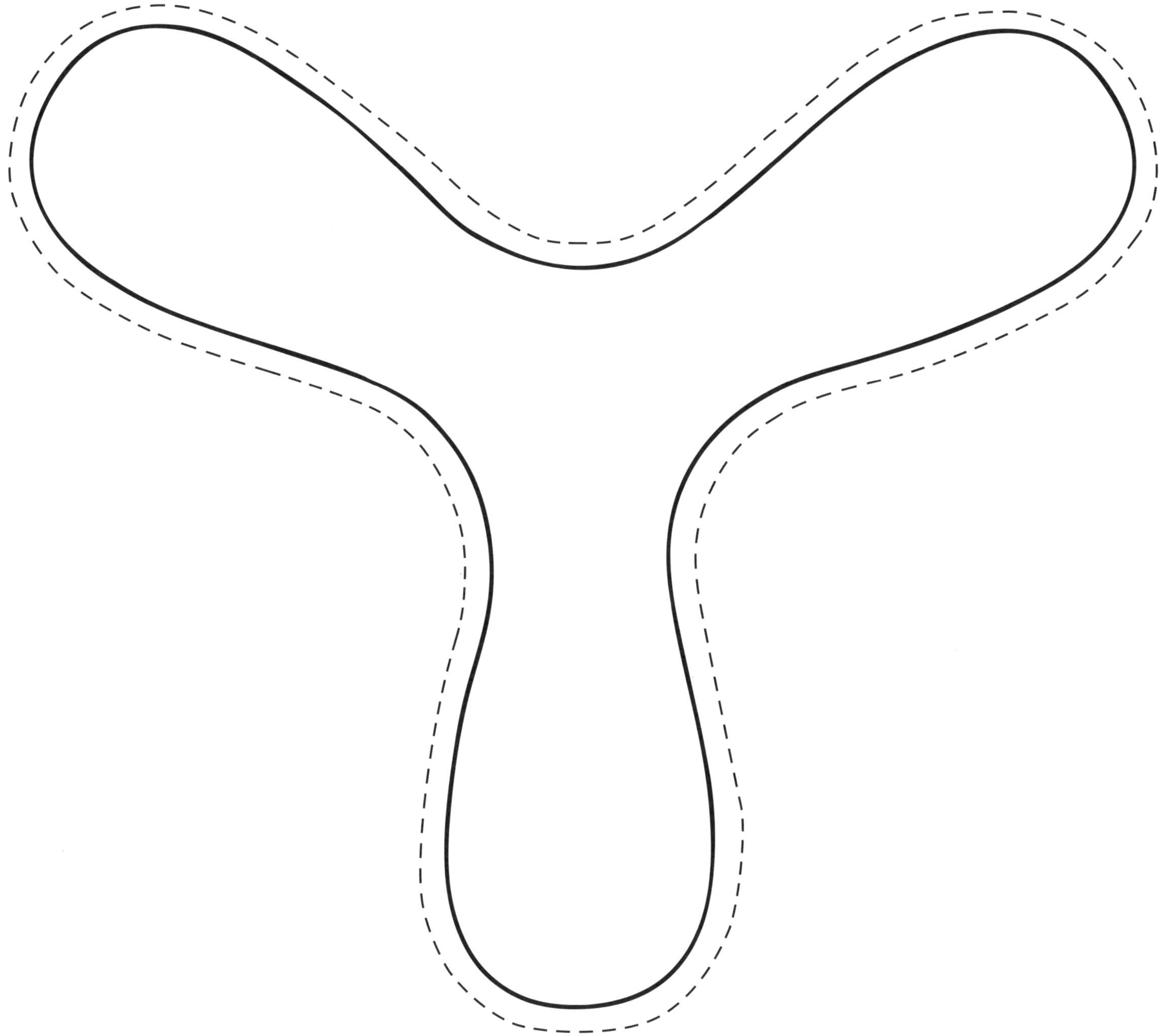

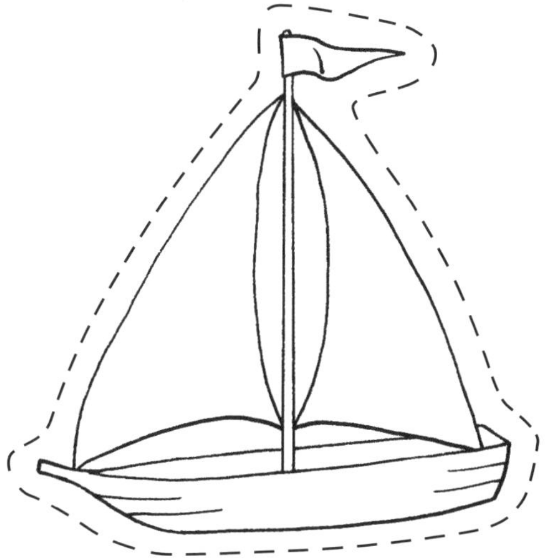
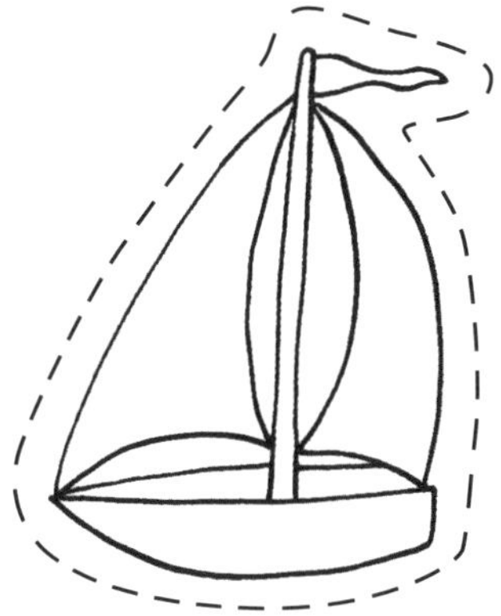
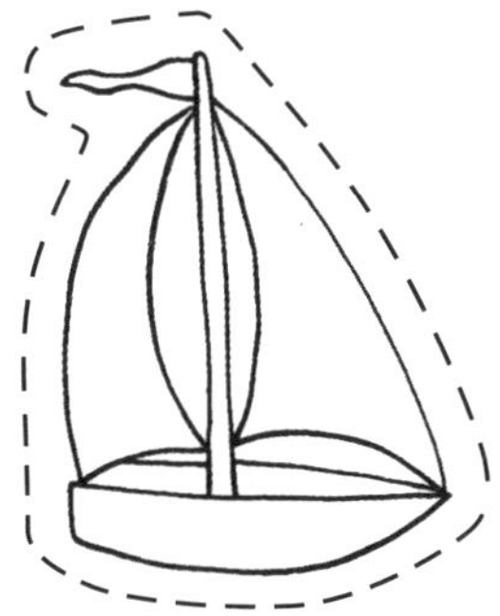
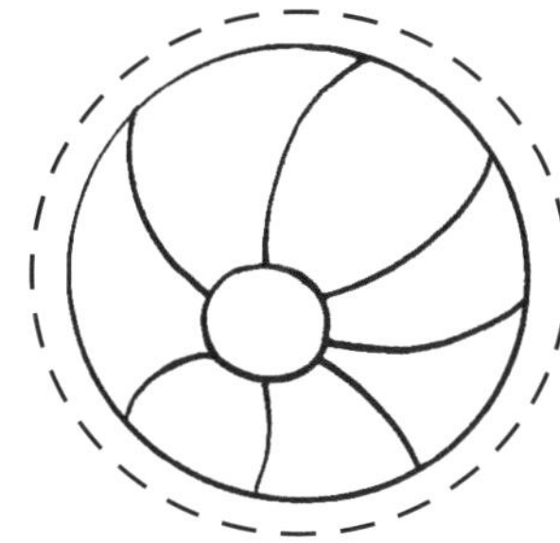
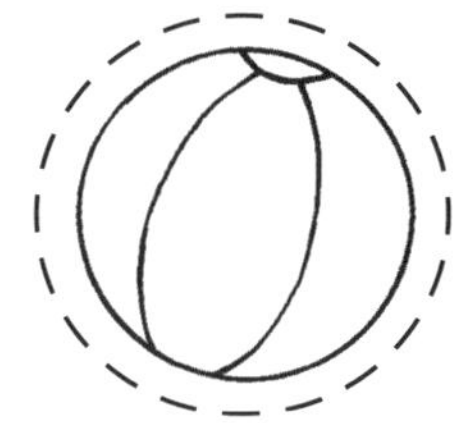
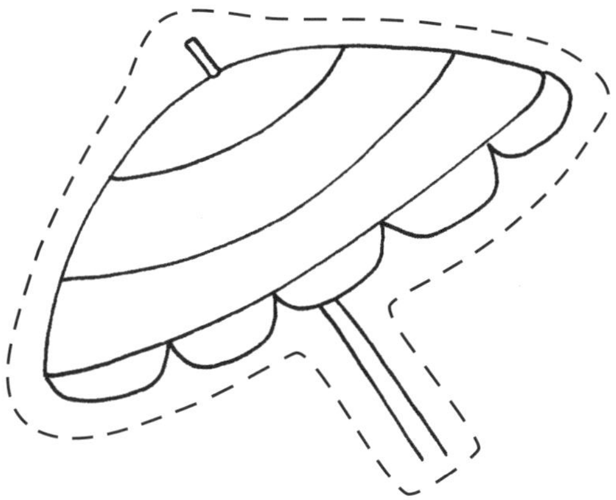
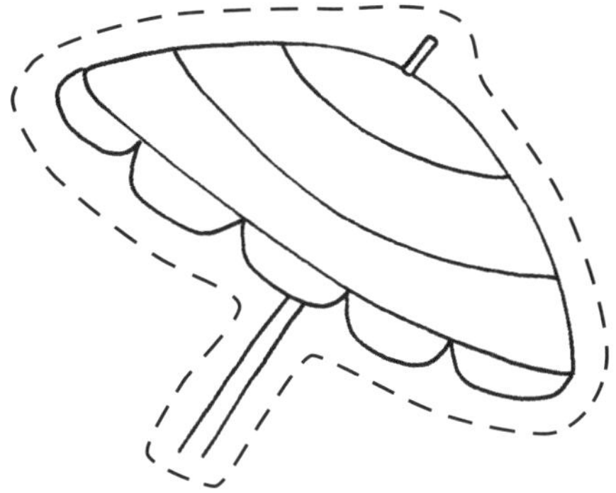
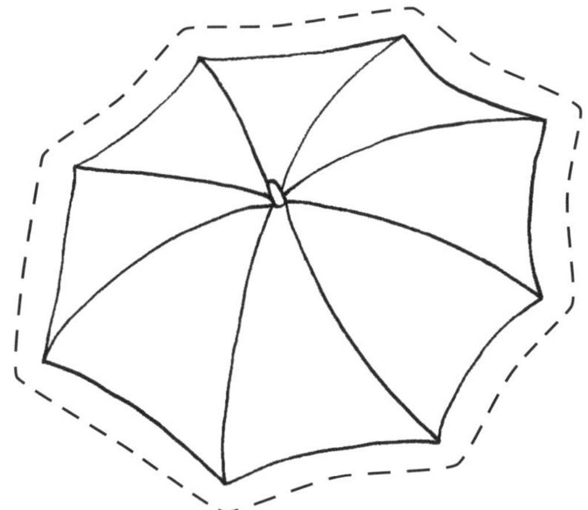

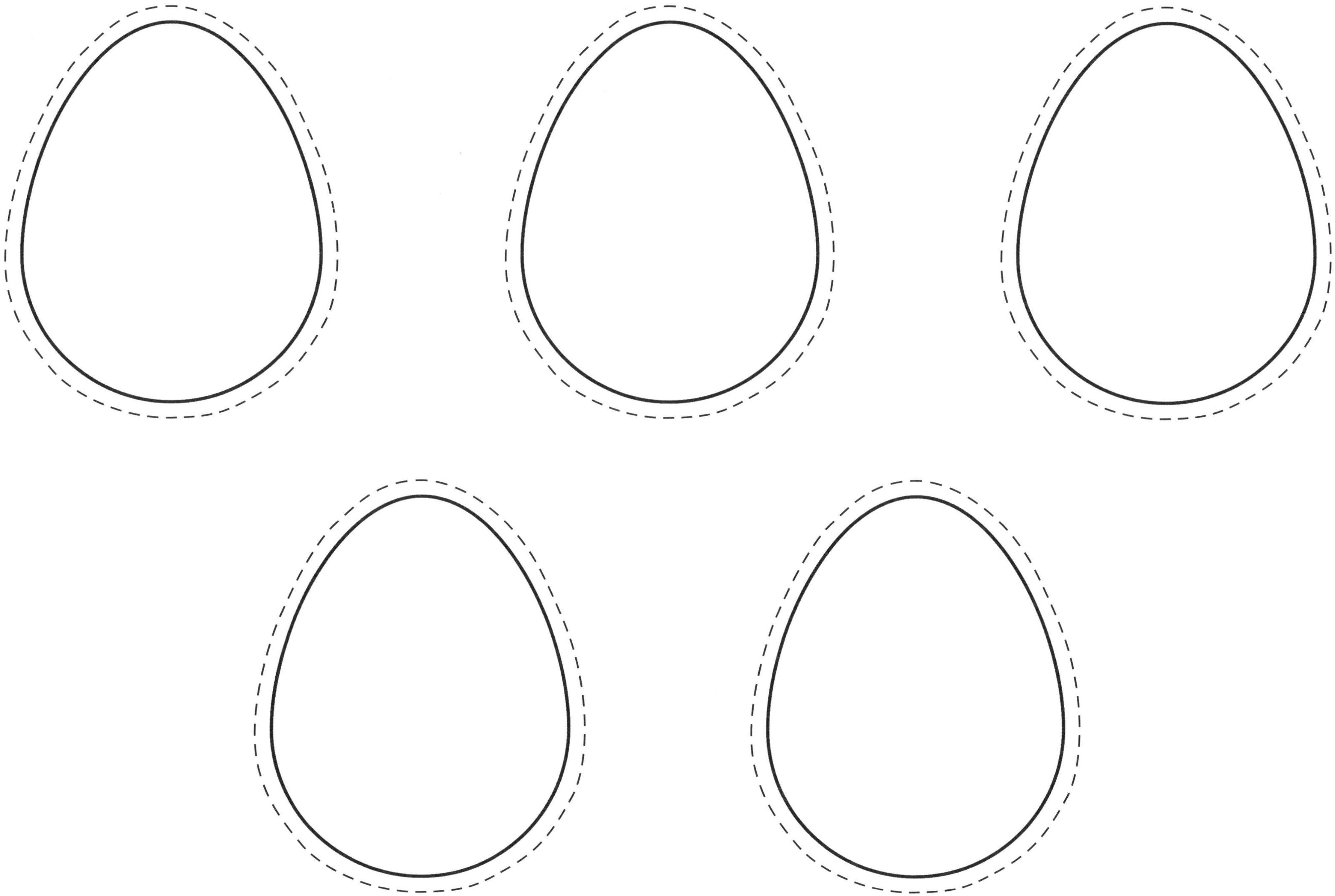